MARY CASSATT

MARY CASSATT

Maria Costantino

BISON GROUP

First published in 1995 by
Bison Books Ltd.
Kimbolton House
117a Fulham Road
London SW3 6RL

ISBN 1-85841-149-1

Printed in Spain

PAGE 1: Mary Cassatt,
photographed in 1914.

PAGE 2: **Young Woman Reading**, 1876
Oil on canvas, 13¾ × 10½ in.
Bequest of John T. Spaulding,
Courtesy, Museum of Fine
Arts, Boston, MA
(48.523)

BELOW: **Summertime**, 1894
Oil on canvas, 28⅞ × 39⅜ in.
Armand Hammer Collection,
U.C.L.A. at Armand Hammer
Museum of Art and Cultural
Center, Los Angeles, CA
(90.9)

CONTENTS

INTRODUCTION

It is only recently that the works of Mary Cassatt have been acknowledged with the due interest and enthusiasm that they deserve, despite the fact that her contemporaries, like the painters Degas and Renoir and the critic J. K. Huysmans, were well aware of her existence and the unique qualities of her work. The main reasons for Cassatt's neglect are: firstly, that women artists have generally been excluded from the mainstream of art history, and their works omitted from exhibitions, simply because they were women. Secondly, Cassatt's nationality placed her generally in the context of nineteenth-century American art, which has only recently been accorded the same interest as that of European art of the same period. Thirdly, as an American artist in France, while Cassatt's style did indeed develop within Impressionism, many art historians who worked according to national categories relegated Cassatt to the fringes of the movement, in spite of the fact that she was a regular exhibitor with the Independents.

Mary Cassatt was born on 23 May 1844 in Allegheny, near Pittsburgh, Pennsylvania, the second daughter of a solidly upper-middle-class family. Her father was a stockbroker, while her mother was an extremely well-educated woman who was widely read and spoke fluent French. In the fall of 1851 the Cassatt family moved to Europe and settled in Paris shortly before Louis Napoleon's coup d'état, when troops occupied the streets of Paris and overran the barricades erected in the city. Hundreds were killed, and it is estimated that 30,000 people were arrested, with a further 10,000 being deported to France's North African colony, Algeria. The Cassatts escaped this turmoil for Germany, where the family remained until 1855, when they returned to America, stopping off in Paris en route to visit the Exposition Universelle.

At the age of 16, Cassatt turned her back on the domestic role which was the normal course for young women of the period, particularly for such a well-educated young lady from a solid Pennsylvanian family with a reasonable fortune. Instead, Cassatt decided to study art seriously. While painting was considered a desirable accomplishment, serious professional study for women was generally frowned upon. Apparently against her father's wishes, Cassatt enrolled at the Pennsylvania Academy of Fine Arts in Philadelphia, where she followed the same course of instruction as her male colleagues, apart from studying the male nude in life classes. For

reasons of "decency," female students were denied access to the male nude, except in the form of plaster casts; thus women artists gained little knowledge of the male figure. This may, in fact, account for the small number of male portraits and figure studies in Cassatt's *oeuvre*. Apart from six portraits and sketches of her father, and 10 of her closest brother, Alexander's, family, only three male portraits exist: the oil *Portrait of Marcellin Desboutins* (1879), and two pastels – the *Portrait of Moïse Dreyfus* (1879), and *Portrait of M.O. de S.* (c. 1909). Furthermore, as a woman of a particular class, Cassatt would not have had access to the worlds frequented by her brothers, and was cut off from the

LEFT: Mary Cassatt as photographed in 1872, at the age of 28.

RIGHT: Mary Cassatt is on the far left of this modeling group at the Pennsylvania Academy of Fine Arts in 1862.

BELOW: Cassatt's *The Bacchante*, painted in 1872 while she was in Italy, clearly shows the influence of Correggio in the modeling of the features, color and pose.

demimonde of bars and brothels. The very streets of Paris were inaccessible to an unchaperoned lady, so the urban scenes which fill the canvases of her French male contemporaries were also ''off limits'' to Cassatt. It is not surprising, therefore, that Cassatt should have turned to the world of women as the subjects for her paintings.

Cassatt remained at the Pennsylvania Academy until 1865, and the following year, accompanied by her classmate Eliza Haldeman, she set off for Europe to study the works of the old masters at first hand. In Paris, Cassatt found the conservative atmosphere of the official art scene exasperating and, with the doors of the Ecole des Beaux-Arts shut firmly against her, she set off to study alone in the museums, also visiting exhibitions such as the Paris Exposition Universelle of 1867, where Courbet and Manet had pavilions.

The outbreak of hostilities between France and Prussia in 1870, and the subsequent civil war in France between 1871 and 1872, obliged Cassatt to return home to Philadelphia, but when peace was restored Cassatt returned to Europe, this time to Italy. In Parma Cassatt concentrated her studies on Correggio (*c.* 1489-1534) and Parmigianino (1503-40), both masters of the theme of the Madonna and child. From Correggio Cassatt learned of draftsmanship and color, while she learned from Parmigianino's complex compositions. From Italy Cassatt traveled to Spain, where she studied the works of Velázquez, in particular his treatment of children in *Las Meninas*. In Madrid she also saw the works of Rubens, and again during a trip to Antwerp.

From 1873 Cassatt regularly exhibited her paintings at the official Paris Salon. *On the Balcony, During Carnival* (1873) was one of Cassatt's first exhibited works, which was submitted – possibly because of her family's disapproval of her chosen career – under the name of Mlle Mary Stevenson. This picture marked the beginning of a series of paintings of Spanish subjects, which include *Spanish Dancer Wearing a Lace Mantilla* (1873), and *Torero and Young Girl* (1873), and which reveal affinities with an artist who was to have a great influence on Cassatt's stylistic development – Edouard Manet. During the 1860s Manet painted several Spanish subjects, many of which Cassatt could have seen in his pavilion at the Exposition Universelle in Paris in 1867.

When Cassatt returned to Paris in 1873, she began working mostly on portraits and single figures, and one recurring theme throughout her work is that of a woman playing a musical instrument. The earliest paintings on this theme are *The Mandolin Player* (c. 1872), and *The Bacchante* (1872), which was painted in Parma and clearly shows the influence of Correggio in both color and pose. In *A Musical Party* (1874), the figures are in contemporary dress, and the picture suggests that Cassatt was now looking seriously at eighteenth-century French painting. The same theme also reappeared in later paintings, like the side panels for the mural *Modern Woman* for the World's Columbian Exposition in Chicago in 1893, and *The Banjo Lesson* (1894).

Cassatt continued to submit paintings to the Paris Salon, and in 1874 she showed her *Portrait of Mme Cartier*, which had been painted in Rome in the same year. This work attracted the attention of Edgar Degas, who is reputed to have commented: "It is real. There is someone who feels as I do." However, it was not until 1877 that Degas was formally introduced to Cassatt by a mutual friend, Joseph Tourney, whom Cassatt had met in Antwerp in 1873.

LEFT: Diego Velázquez's *Las Meninas*, of 1656. His treatment of children in this painting fascinated Cassatt.

RIGHT: Cassatt's *Portrait of a Woman*, 1872 (oil on canvas, 23 × 19¾ in.) was painted during a period in which she liked to concentrate on the study of individuals.

In 1875 one of Cassatt's paintings, possibly *La Jeune Mariée (The Young Bride)* (*c.* 1875), was rejected by the Salon for being too highly colored. The sitter for this painting has been identified as Cassatt's maid, Martha Ganloser, who is depicted knitting peacefully. The dress and activity of the model reveal the influence of Cassatt's visit to the Low Countries, where she had, no doubt, seen similar themes depicted by many Dutch painters. It is also possible that she had seen Vermeer's *The Lacemaker*, which had been purchased by the Louvre in around 1870. Another of her works that is stylistically close to *La Jeune Mariée* is *Young Girl with a Portfolio of Pictures* (*c.* 1876), which is also one of the few representations of children to be found in the first decade of Cassatt's work.

By the mid-1870s Cassatt was turning away from the picturesque themes of her early works, and was beginning to concentrate on painting subjects drawn from the life around her. *Mrs. Duffee Seated on a Striped Sofa* (1876) marks a turning point in her work: the color, the interior setting, and the occupation of the sitter now show the influence of French eighteenth-century artists, in particular Jean-Honoré Fragonard (1732-1806) – an influence which was shared by the Impressionists. The portrait of Mrs. Duffee is also one of Cassatt's earliest paintings on the theme of women reading: this subject reappears in *The Reader* (1877); in portraits of Cassatt's sister, such as *Lydia Reading the Morning Paper* (1878), and *Lydia Reading in a Garden* (1880); and of her mother, in *Reading Le Figaro* (1878). More usual feminine activities, such as crocheting, as seen in *Lydia Crocheting in the Garden at Marly* (1880), or needle-work, as in *Lydia at a Tapestry Frame* (*c.* 1881), taking tea and visiting, such as in *Five O'Clock Tea* (1880), and *Lady at a Tea Table* (1885), form the major part of Cassatt's work from the mid-1870s to the mid-1880s.

In 1877 Cassatt's Salon entry was rejected, but that year Degas visited her, and invited her to join the

Independents — an exhibiting society which had been founded in 1874, and whose members had become known as the Impressionists. Cassatt first exhibited with the group in 1879, showing two works: *The Cup of Tea* (1879), and *Woman with a Pearl Necklace in a Loge* (1879). Cassatt's family had returned to Paris in 1877, and her sister Lydia frequently served as her model until her early death in 1882. *Woman with a Pearl Necklace in a Loge*, which is also known as *Lydia in a Loge Wearing a Pearl Necklace*, placed Cassatt immediately within the Impressionist group; compositionally it recalls Renoir's painting, *The Loge* (1874), which had been shown at the first Impressionist exhibition in 1874. Cassatt's portrait of her sister is one of the first works in a series of oils, pastels and etchings set in a theater that include *Lydia Leaning on her Arms, Seated in a Loge* (c. 1879), *Young Woman in a Loge Holding a Wide-Open Fan* (1879), *Woman in Black at the Opera* (1880), and *Two Young Ladies in a Loge* (1882). For this last painting the models were Genevieve, the daughter of the poet Stéphane Mallarmé (1842-98), and Miss Mary Ellison, whose

portrait Cassatt had already painted a few years earlier, in about 1880.

In 1880 Cassatt's brother, Alexander, arrived in Paris with his young family. Their arrival renewed Cassatt's interest in depicting children, and her nephews and nieces now provided the opportunity for Cassatt to study and paint children from life. Taking advantage of her brother's family as models, Cassatt produced such works as the double portrait, *Portrait of Mr. Alexander J. Cassatt and his Son, Robert Kelso* (1884).

One of Cassatt's earliest works on the theme of the mother and child, *Mother About to Wash her Sleepy Child* (1880), is one in which Cassatt brought together her experiments in Impressionistic brushwork and color, particularly in the use of the complementaries of red and green, and in the way the green of the chair affects the local color of the white dress. But it was in 1889 that Cassatt began the most intensive series of works on this theme, beginning with the unfinished canvas, *Emmie and her Child* (1889). While mother and child do not look at each other, they are linked by the physical bond

RIGHT: Degas as an elderly man, pictured in the Parisian streets.

created by the child's hand on its mother's face while she, in turn, clasps her child's leg. The child's gesture is repeated in the pastel *Baby's First Caress* (1891). Because of the appearance here, and in the later painting *Mother and Child (The Oval Mirror)* (1901), of a nude boy-child, and especially because this painting uses the device of the mirror frame to act as a sort of halo, these works have been seen as contemporary forms of the Madonna and child. Yet any lasting association of Cassatt with this tradition is countered by the fact that the majority of her

works on the mother-and-child theme are representations of mothers and their daughters. It has also been suggested that rather than these works being modern reworkings of the Madonna-and-child motif, Cassatt instead used the parent and child to express one of the phases of family life which starts with babyhood. This can be seen in *After the Bath* (1901), *Ellen Mary Cassatt in a White Coat* (c. 1896), and *The Bath* (1891-92); moving on through the early years of life in *The Sisters* (c. 1885); to adolescence, in *Girl Arranging*

RIGHT: The mother-and-child theme was one that Cassatt never tired of. *La Lecture* of 1898 was a pastel variation on the subject.

Her Hair (1886), and Summertime (1894); through to the mature young woman in Susan on a Balcony Holding a Dog (c. 1880), or Portrait of a Young Woman in Black (1883); and finally depicting the later stages of female life in the portraits of Cassatt's own mother.

During her stay in Parma in 1872, Cassatt had taken lessons in basic etching techniques from Carlo Raimondi. In 1880, when Cassatt was invited by Degas to contribute to the journal Le Jour et La Nuit, her interest in the medium was revived. As a contribution to the journal, Cassatt worked on In The Opera Box (No.3), another version of the "loge paintings." In her first attempts at printmaking, Cassatt worked in soft ground and aquatint, which allowed for the subtle shading that is apparent in works like The Visitor (1881), and Before the Fireplace (c. 1883). Cassatt often worked on her prints at home in the evening, and the softly lamplit interiors were often the subject of her prints. Later Cassatt turned to another technique – drypoint – and, by 1890, the chiaroscuro of her soft-ground etchings had given way to drypoint compositions where the clarity of line plays a more important role.

ABOVE: Degas's print, The Washbasin, which shares many characteristics with Cassatt's work, including theme and style. Both artists were influenced by an exhibition of Japanese prints in 1890.

RIGHT: By 1890 Cassatt was regularly using the technique of drypoint. This example is called Jeannette Wearing a Bonnet (1904).

OPPOSITE PAGE: Renoir's La Loge, 1874 (oil on canvas, 31½ × 24¾ in.) was shown at the first Impressionist exhibition in 1874, and inspired Cassatt's series of "loge paintings."

In the same year there was a major exhibition at the Ecole des Beaux-Arts of Japanese prints of the Ukiyo-e school of the eighteenth and nineteenth centuries. These woodcut prints, in which areas of intense, unmodulated color were combined with elegant lines and an unusual perspective or angle of vision, were to become the basis for many experiments in oils by Manet, Degas, Monet and Cassatt. However, the approach and methods of the Japanese printmakers were best assimilated into the graphic arts, and in response Cassatt set up her own

LEFT: Paul Durand-Ruel, an art dealer who specialized in the work of the Impressionists, and who exhibited Cassatt's work in solo shows in Paris in 1893 and in New York in 1895.

press, producing a series of color prints in 1891. Of these, *The Omnibus* takes as its subject a typical scene from modern city life, while *The Letter* has been directly compared with Utamuaro's *Portrait of Oiran Hinzauro* (*c.* 1796). Like the Japanese printmakers, Cassatt juxtaposed areas of pure color with richly patterned surfaces. Yet, for many, the most remarkable aspect of Cassatt's prints is the technique: drypoint for the design, aquatint for the patterns, and soft-ground etching to achieve the textured effects of the color areas.

In 1893 the World's Columbian Exposition was held in Chicago, where there was a special Women's Building, designed by Sophia Hayden. As one of the most successful women artists, Cassatt was commissioned to paint a mural for the tympanum of the Great Hall, on the theme of "Modern Women." The completed work has been lost, but it has been suggested that other paintings, such as *Women Picking Fruit* (1891), are possibly related.

In 1895 Cassatt had a large solo show in New York, which was organized by Durand-Ruel. The majority of the works on show had already been exhibited earlier, in 1893, at a solo show in Durand-Ruel's Paris gallery.

After an absence of more than 25 years, in 1898 Cassatt made her first trip back to the United States. Despite her quarter-century as a professional artist, with major exhibitions and recognition in Europe to her name, the *Philadelphia Ledger* announced Cassatt's return home with a brief note: "Mary Cassatt, sister of Mr. Cassatt, President of the Pennsylvania Railroad, returned from Europe yesterday. She has been studying painting in France and owns the smallest Pekinese dog in the world." The *Ledger*'s somewhat cursory observation of

Cassatt's talent was not truly representative of American opinion, for within the American avant-garde artistic world Cassatt's reputation had, in fact, grown substantially over the years during which she was absent from America. She was now recognized in her home country as being a major artist, and worthy of being ranked alongside her male compatriots Whistler, Sargent, Homer, and Eakins. Yet Cassatt was to remain fiercely independent of the official art scene in America. Cynical of jury systems, she refused to submit paintings for shows where the works were selected by such arbiters of taste. In 1904 she declined an award of $300 from the Pennsylvania Academy of Fine Arts for a pastel of a mother and child, claiming that, as a member of the Independents, she had to stick by her principles: no juries, no medals, and no awards. Nevertheless, in the same year she was awarded the highest honor that her adopted country of France could bestow on her: the *Légion d'honneur*, awarded to a woman artist for only the second time in its history.

In 1910 Cassatt made her last trip abroad, this time to the Near East and to Egypt. In the same year she became openly associated with the early feminist movement, under the leadership of Carrie Chapman Catt, and later, in 1915, she exhibited with Degas in a benefit exhibition for women's suffrage at the Knoedler Gallery in New York. By this time, however, Cassatt was in poor health: in 1911 she had experienced the shock of the death of her brother, Gardner, and suffered a physical and nervous breakdown, after which diabetes was diagnosed. As her eyesight began to be weakened by cataracts, Cassatt was forced to give up printmaking and, despite numerous operations to remove the cataracts in 1915, and later in 1921, Cassatt became virtually blind, and could no longer continue painting. On 14 June 1926 Mary Cassatt, aged 82, died at her home at the Château de Beaufresne, at Mesnil-Theribus in her beloved France.

BELOW: Edgar Degas's *Portrait of Mary Cassatt, c. 1880-84.*

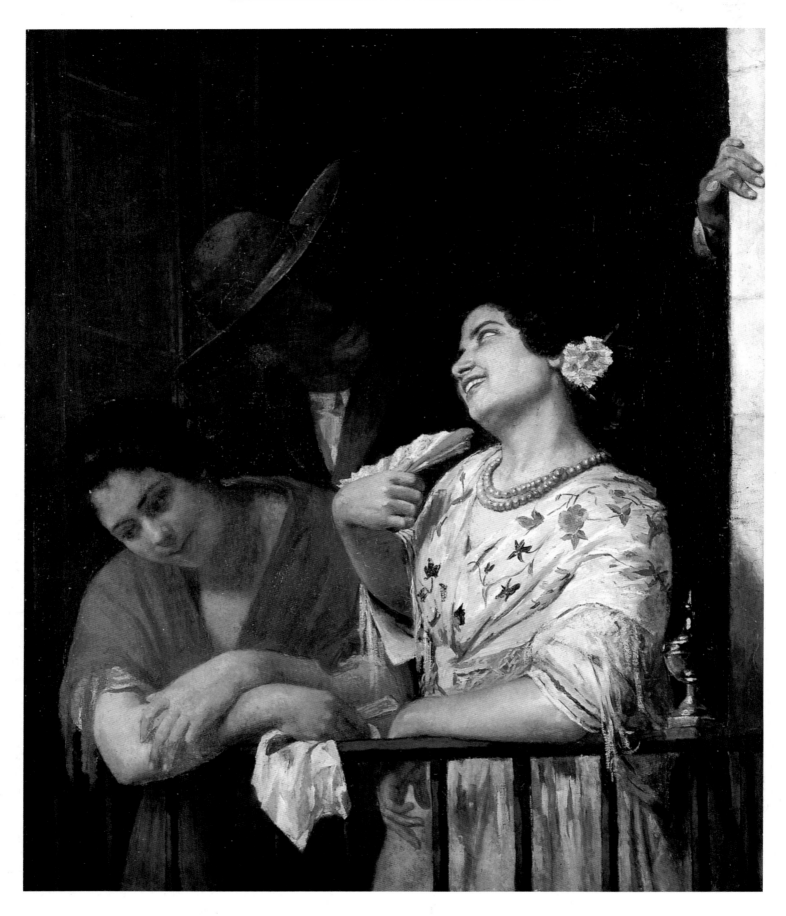

On the Balcony, During Carnival, 1873
Oil on canvas, 39¾ × 32½ in.
W. P. Wilstach Collection,
Philadelphia Museum of Art, PA
(W'06-1-7)

Toreador, 1873
Oil on canvas, 32⅛ × 25³⁄₁₆ in.
Gift of Mrs. Sterling Morton,
© 1994 The Art Institute of Chicago, IL
All Rights Reserved.
(1969.332)

ABOVE:
Offering the *Panal* to the Toreador, 1873
Oil on canvas, 39⅝ × 33½ in.
Sterling and Francine Clark Art Institute,
Williamstown, MA
(# 1)

RIGHT:
A Musical Party, 1874
Oil on canvas, 38 × 26 in.
Musée du Petit Palais, Paris

18

LEFT:
Young Woman Reading, 1876
Oil on canvas, 13¾ × 10½ in.
Bequest of John T. Spaulding,
Courtesy, Museum of Fine Arts, Boston, MA
(48.523)

ABOVE:
Mary Ellison Embroidering, 1877
Oil on canvas, 29¼ × 23½ in.
Gift of the Children of Jean Thompson Thayer,
Philadelphia Museum of Art, PA
(1986-108-1)

Head of a Young Girl, before 1878
Oil on panel, 12¾ × 9 in.
Gift of Walter Gay,
Courtesy, Museum of Fine Arts, Boston, MA
(27.497)

Reading *Le Figaro*, 1878
Oil on canvas, 39¹⁄₁₆ × 34¼ in.
Christie's, London

Little Girl in a Blue Armchair, 1878
Oil on canvas, 35¼ × 51⅛ in.
Collection of Mr. and Mrs. Paul Mellon,
© 1994 Board of Trustees, National Gallery of Art,
Washington, DC (1983.1.18)

LEFT:
Self-Portrait, *c.* 1878
Gouache on paper, 23½ × 17½ in.
Bequest of Edith H. Proskauer,
The Metropolitan Museum of Art, New York, NY
(1975.319.1)

ABOVE:
The Cup of Tea, 1879
Oil on canvas, 36⅜ × 25¾ in.
From the Collection of James Stillman,
Gift of Dr. Ernest G. Stillman, 1922,
The Metropolitan Museum of Art, New York, NY
(22.16.17)

In the Loge, *c.* 1879
Pastel and metallic paint on canvas, 26⅝ × 32 in.
Gift of Margaret Sargent McKean,
Philadelphia Museum of Art, PA
('50-52-1)

At the Theater (Woman in a Loge), *c.* 1879
Pastel on paper, 21^{13}/$_{16}$ × 18^{1}/$_{8}$ in.
Purchase: Acquired Through the Generosity
of an Anonymous Donor,
The Nelson-Atkins Museum of Art, Kansas City, MO
(F77-33)

Portrait of Moïse Dreyfus, 1879
Pastel on paper mounted on canvas, 31½ × 25 in.
Musée du Petit Palais, Paris

31

RIGHT:
Miss Mary Ellison, *c.* 1880
Oil on canvas, 33¾ × 25⅝ in.
Chester Dale Collection,
© 1994 Board of Trustees,
National Gallery of Art, Washington, DC
(1963.10.95)

ABOVE:
Profile Portrait of Lydia, 1880
Oil on canvas, 36½ × 25½ in.
Musée du Petit Palais, Paris

Lydia Crocheting in the Garden at Marly, 1880
Oil on canvas, 26 × 37 in.
Gift of Mrs. Gardner Cassatt, 1965,
The Metropolitan Museum of Art, New York, NY
(65.184)

Five O'Clock Tea, 1880
Oil on canvas, 25½ × 36½ in.
M. Theresa B. Hopkins Fund,
Courtesy, Museum of Fine Arts, Boston, MA
(42.178)

Woman Reading in a Garden, 1880
Oil on canvas, 35½ × 25⅝ in.
Gift of Mrs. Albert J. Beveridge
in Memory of her Aunt, Delia Spencer Field,
© 1994 The Art Institute of Chicago, IL
All Rights Reserved.
(1938.18)

At the Opera, 1880
Oil on canvas, 31½ × 25½ in.
The Hayden Collection
Courtesy, Museum of Fine Arts, Boston, MA
(10.35)

39

LEFT:
Susan on a Balcony Holding a Dog, *c.* 1880
Oil on canvas, 39½ × 25½ in.
Museum Purchase, Gallery Fund,
In the Collection of the Corcoran Gallery of Art,
Washington, DC
(09.8)

ABOVE:
Portrait of a Young Woman in Black, 1883
Oil on canvas, 31½ × 25¼ in.
The Peabody Institute of the City of Baltimore,
On Extended Loan to the Baltimore Museum of Art, MD
(BMA L.1964.18)

PAGES 42-43:
Woman and Child Driving, 1881
Oil on canvas, 35¼ × 51½ in.
W. P. Wilstach Collection,
Philadelphia Museum of Art, PA
(W'21-1-1)

RIGHT:
Lydia at a Tapestry Frame, c. 1881
Oil on canvas, 25¾ × 36¼ in.
Gift of the Whiting Foundation,
Flint Institute of Arts, MI
(67.32)

LEFT:
Femme Cousante
(Young Woman Sewing in the Garden), *c.* 1880-82
Oil on canvas, 36 × 25½ in.
Musée d'Orsay, Paris

ABOVE:
Portrait of Mr. Alexander J. Cassatt and his Son,
Robert Kelso, 1884-85
Oil on canvas, 39½ × 32 in.
The W. P. Wilstach Collection,
Philadelphia Museum of Art, PA
(W'59-1-1)

Children Playing on the Beach, 1884
Oil on canvas, 38⅜ × 29¼ in.
Ailsa Mellon Bruce Collection,
© 1994 Board of Trustees,
National Gallery of Art, Washington, DC
(1970.17.19)

Lady at the Tea Table, 1885
Oil on canvas, 29 × 24 in.
Gift of the Artist, 1923,
The Metropolitan Museum of Art, New York, NY
(23.101)

The Sisters, *c.* 1885
Oil on canvas, 18¼ × 21¹⁵/₁₆ in.
Glasgow Museums: Art Gallery and Museum,
Kelvingrove 2980

51

Child in a Straw Hat, *c.* 1886
Oil on canvas, 25¾ × 19½ in.
Collection of Mr. and Mrs. Paul Mellon,
National Gallery of Art, Washington, DC
(1983.1.17)

Girl Arranging Her Hair, 1886
Oil on canvas, 29⅝ × 24⅝ in.
Chester Dale Collection,
© 1994 Board of Trustees,
National Gallery of Art, Washington, DC
(1963.10.97)

Patty Cake, 1897
Pastel on paper, 23¾ × 28¼ in.
Denver Art Museum, CO
(1986.729)

LEFT:

**Mrs. Robert S. Cassatt, the Artist's Mother
(Katharine Kelso Johnson Cassatt),** *c.* 1889
Oil on canvas, 38 × 27 in.
Museum Purchase, William H. Noble Bequest Fund,
The Fine Arts Museums of San Francisco, CA
(1979.35)

ABOVE:
Mother and Child, 1889
Oil on canvas, 29 × 23½ in.
John J. Emery Endowment,
Cincinnati Art Museum, OH
(1928.222)

LEFT:
Hélène de Septeuil, 1889
Pastel on beige paper, 25⅞ × 16½ in.
Louise Crombie Beach Memorial Collection,
The William Benton Museum of Art,
The University of Connecticut, Storrs, CT
(1948.1)

ABOVE:
Jeune Femme à la Fenêtre *or* **A la Fenêtre,** *c.* 1890
Pastel and charcoal on gray-beige paper, 29⅓ × 24⅔ in.
Musée d'Orsay, Paris

On the Water, early 1890s
Oil on canvas, 23¾ × 28¾ in.
Private Collection, Chevy Chase, MD

Afternoon Tea Party (Third State), *c.* 1891
Drypoint and aquatint in color on paper, 13⅝ × 10½ in.
Gift of Paul J. Sachs, 1917,
The Metropolitan Museum of Art, New York, NY
(16.2.1)

The Child's Caress, *c.* 1891
Oil on canvas, 25½ × 19¾ in.
Gift in Memory of Wilhemina Tenney, 1953,
Honolulu Academy of Arts, HI
(HAA 1855.1)

ABOVE:
The Family, *c.* 1892
Oil on canvas, 32¼ × 26⅛ in.
Gift of Walter P. Chrysler, Jr.
The Chrysler Museum, Norfolk, VA
(71.498)

ABOVE:
In the Garden, 1893
Pastel, 28¾ × 25⅝ in.
The Cone Collection, Formed by Dr. Claribel Cone
and Miss Etta Cone of Baltimore, Maryland,
The Baltimore Museum of Art, MD
(BMA 1950.193)

RIGHT:
Baby Reaching for an Apple, 1893
Oil on canvas, 39½ × 25¾ in.
Gift of an Anonymous Donor,
Virginia Museum of Fine Arts, Richmond, VA
(75.18)

The Boating Party, 1893-94
Oil on canvas, 35⁷⁄₁₆ × 46⅛ in.
© 1994 Board of Trustees,
National Gallery of Art, Washington, DC
(1963.10.94)

Summertime, 1894
Oil on canvas, 28⅞ × 39⅜ in.
Armand Hammer Collection,
U.C.L.A. at Armand Hammer
Museum of Art and Cultural
Center, Los Angeles, CA
(90.9)

Summertime, *c.* 1894
Oil on canvas, 39⅝ × 32 in.
Terra Foundation for the Arts, Daniel J. Terra Collection,
Terra Museum of American Art, Chicago, IL
(1988.25)

Gathering Fruit (Final State), *c.* 1895
Drypoint and color aquatint on paper, 16¾ × 11¾ in.
Rogers Fund, 1918,
The Metropolitan Museum of Art, New York, NY
(18.33.4)

Nurse Reading to a Little Girl, 1895
Pastel on paper, 23¾ × 27⅞ in.
Gift of Mrs. Hope Williams Read, 1962,
The Metropolitan Museum of Art, New York, NY
(62.72)

Maternal Caress, *c.* 1896
Oil on canvas, 15 × 21¼ in.
Gift of Aaron Carpenter,
Philadelphia Museum of Art, PA
('70-75-2)

A Kiss for Baby Anne, *c.* 1897
Pastel on paper, 21½ × 18¼ in.
The Helen and Abram Eisenberg Collection,
The Baltimore Museum of Art, MD
(BMA 1976.55.1)

Louisine W. Havemeyer, 1896
Pastel on paper, 29 × 24 in.
Courtesy of Shelburne Museum, VT
(27.3.1-19)

Women Admiring a Child, 1897
Pastel on paper, 26 × 32 in.
Gift of Edward Chandler Walker,
© Detroit Institute of Arts, MI
(08.8)

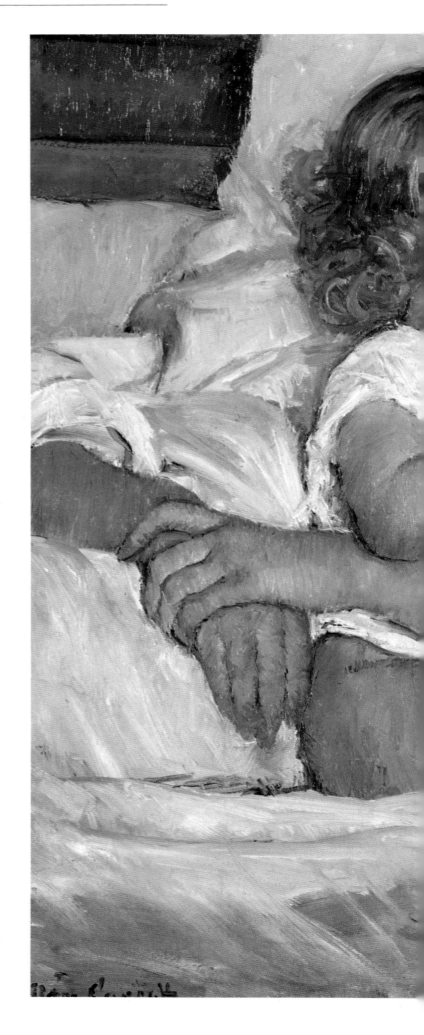

Breakfast in Bed, 1897
Oil on canvas, 23 × 29 in.
Virginia Steel Scott Collection,
Henry E. Huntington Library and Art Gallery,
San Marino, CA
(83.8.6)

PAGES 92-93:
Mother Feeding her Child, 1898
Pastel, 25½ × 32 in.
From the Collection of James Stillman,
Gift of Dr. Ernest G. Stillman, 1922,
The Metropolitan Museum of Art, New York, NY
(22.16.22)

LEFT:
Mother Playing With Her Child, 1898
Pastel on paper, 25½ × 31½ in.
From the Collection of James Stillman,
Gift of Dr. Ernest G. Stillman, 1922,
The Metropolitan Museum of Art, New York, NY
(22.16.23)

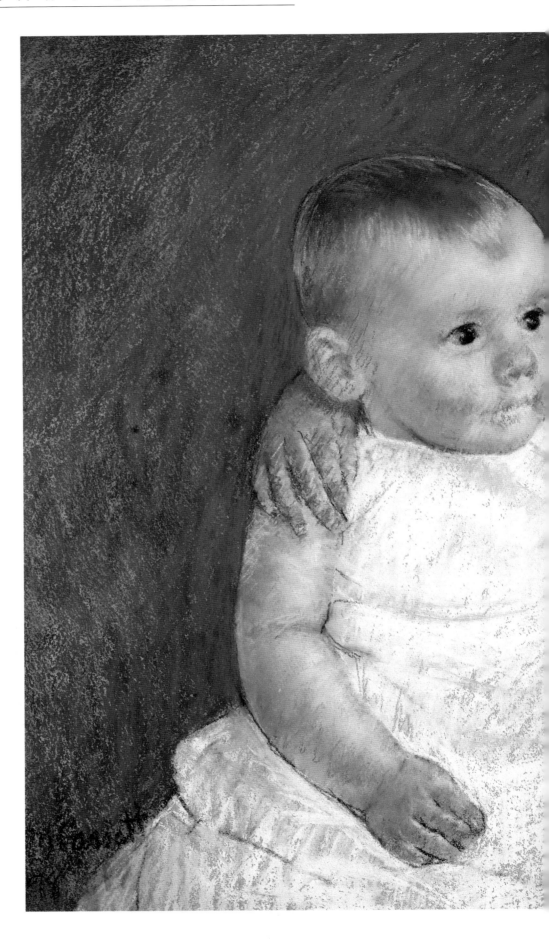

**Portrait of Gardiner Hammond
and George F. Hammond,** 1898.
Pastel on paper, 20 × 24½ in. (mat window)
Collection of Mrs. George Fiske Hammond,
Montecito, CA

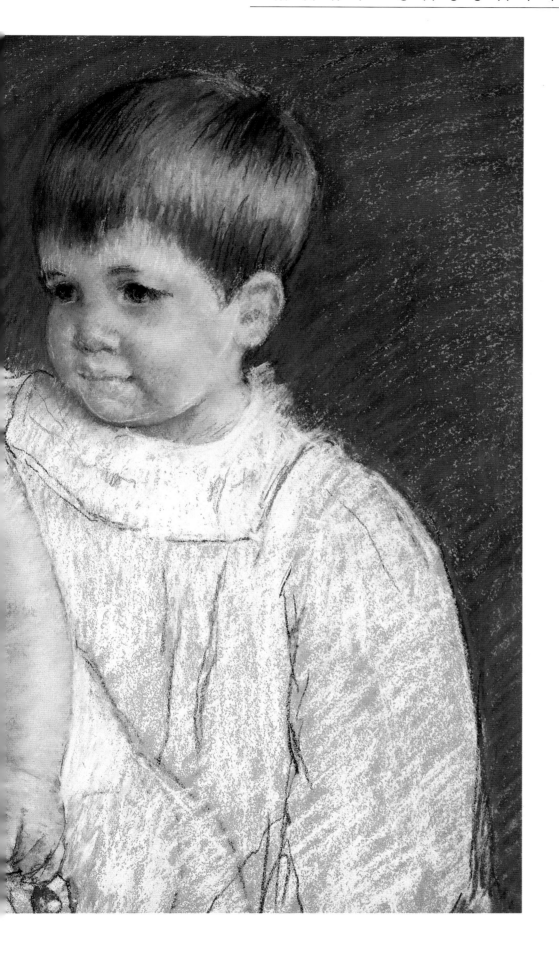

ABOVE:
Portrait of Gardiner Hammond, 1898 (?)
Pastel on paper, 20 × 24½ in. (mat window)
Collection of Mrs. George Fiske Hammond,
Montecito, CA

RIGHT:
Young Mother Sewing, *c.* 1900
Oil on canvas, 36⅜ × 29 in.
Bequest of Mrs. H. O. Havemeyer, 1929,
The H. O. Havemeyer Collection,
The Metropolitan Museum of Art, New York, NY
(29.100.48)

LEFT:
Mother and Child, 1900
Oil on canvas, 27⅛ × 20⅜ in.
Carll H. De Silver Fund,
The Brooklyn Museum, NY
(19.95)

ABOVE:
Mother and Two Children, 1901
Oil on canvas, tondo, 37½ in.
Anonymous Gift,
Collection of the Westmorland Museum of Art,
Greensburg, PA
(79.1)

Mother Combing her Child's Hair, *c.* 1901
Pastel and gouache on tan paper, 25¼ × 31⅗ in.
Bequest of Mary T. Cockcroft,
The Brooklyn Museum, NY
(46.102)

After the Bath, 1901
Pastel, 23⅗ × 39¼ in.
Gift of J. H. Wade,
The Cleveland Museum of Art, OH
(20.379)

ABOVE:
Mother and Child (The Oval Mirror), 1901
Oil on canvas, 32⅛ × 25⅞ in.
Bequest of Mrs H. O. Havemeyer, 1929,
The H. O. Havemeyer Collection,
The Metropolitan Museum of Art, New York, NY
(29.100.47)

RIGHT:
Margot in Blue, 1902
Pastel on heavy paper, light canvas back, 24 × 19¾ in.
The Walters Art Gallery, Baltimore, MD
(37.303)

In the Garden, 1904
Oil on canvas, 26¾ × 32½ in.
Gift of Dr. Ernest G. Stillman,
© The Detroit Institute of Arts, MI
(22.6)

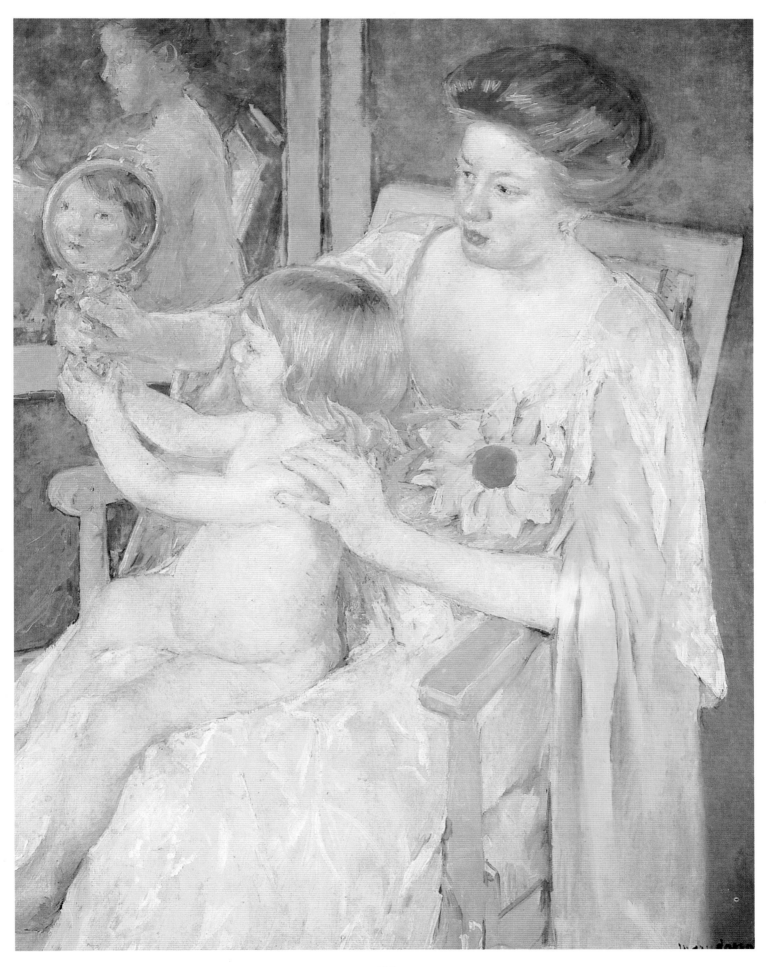

Family Group Reading (A Garden Lecture), *c.* 1901
Oil on canvas, 22¼ × 44¼ in.
Given by Mr. and Mrs. J. Watson Webb,
Philadelphia Museum of Art, PA
('42-102-1)

112

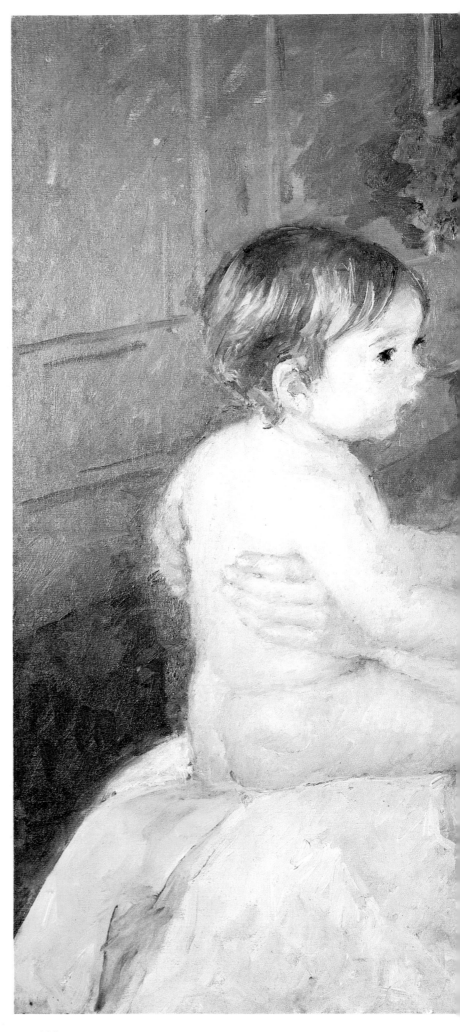

Woman and Children, 1906
Oil on canvas, 29¼ × 36¼ in.
Gift of Dr. Ernest G. Stillman,
Courtesy of the Fogg Art Museum,
Harvard University, Cambridge, MA
(1922.28)

114

LEFT:
Ellen Mary Cassatt in a Big Blue Hat, *c.* 1905
Oil on canvas, 40¼ × 31½ in.
Collection of Dr. Herchel Smith, 1977
Courtesy of the Williams College Museum of Art,
Williams College, Williamstown, MA
(EL.77.1.1)

ABOVE:
Françoise in Green, Sewing, *c.* 1908
Oil on canvas, 32 × 25½ in.
Gift of Dr. Ernest G. Stillman,
The Saint Louis Art Museum, MO
(1:1922)

117

LEFT:
Mother and Child, 1908
Oil on canvas, 32 × 23⅞ in.
Alex Simpson, Jr. Collection,
Philadelphia Museum of Art, PA
(1928-63-3)

ABOVE:
Fillette au Grand Chapeau, c. 1908
Pastel on buff paper, 25¼ × 19½ in.
Henry E. Huntington Library and Art Gallery,
San Marino, CA
(26.125)

Sleepy Baby, *c.* 1910
Pastel on paper, 25½ × 20½ in.
Munger Fund,
Dallas Museum of Art, TX
(1952.38M)

La Jeune Fille, *c.* 1910
Oil on canvas, 16¾ × 14½ in.
Gift of Mrs. Henry C. Woods,
© 1994 The Art Institute of Chicago, IL
All Rights Reserved.
(1964.1099)

Portrait of Charles Dikran Kelekian at Age 12, 1910
Pastel on paper, 36½ × 21⅛ in.
Bequest of Beatrice A. Kelekian in memory of Mr. and Mrs.
Charles D. Kelekian
The Walters Art Gallery, Baltimore, MD
(37.2656)

Mother and Child, n.d.
Pastel on paper, 28 × 23 in.
Bequest of John J. Ireland,
© 1994 The Art Institute of Chicago, IL
All Rights Reserved.
(1968.81)

**Two Mothers and Their Nude
Children in a Boat,** 1910
Oil on canvas, 39 × 50¾ in.
Musée du Petit Palais, Paris,

ABOVE:
Two Sisters (Study for the Banjo Lesson), n.d.
Pastel on paper, 17 × 17 in.
The Hayden Collection,
Courtesy, Museum of Fine Arts, Boston, MA
(32.98)

RIGHT:
Mother and Child, n .d.
Oil on canvas, 36½ × 29 in.
Gift of Miss Aimée Lamb,
In Memory of Mr. and Mrs. Horatio A. Lamb,
Courtesy, Museum of Fine Arts, Boston, MA
(1970.252)

ACKNOWLEDGMENTS

The publisher would like to thank Martin Bristow, the designer; Sara Dunphy and Suzanne O'Farrell, the picture researchers; Clare Haworth-Maden, the editor; Simon Shelmerdine for production; and the museums and individuals listed below for supplying the illustrations.

Archives of American Art, Smithsonian Institution, NY/Frederick A. Sweet Papers (Photograph Courtesy of the Chicago Art Institute): page 1

The Baltimore Museum of Art, MD/The Cone Collection, formed by Dr. Claribel Cone and Miss Etta Cone of Baltimore, MD: page 74/The Helen and Abram Eisenberg Collection: page 86

The William Benton Museum of Art, The University of Connecticut, Storrs, CT/Louise Crombie Beach Memorial Collection: page 58

Bibliothèque Nationale, Paris: page 11(top)

The Bridgeman Art Library/Christie's, London: page 23

Brooklyn Museum, NY/Carll H. De Silver Fund: page 100/Bequest of Mary T. Cockcroft: pages 102-103

© 1994 The Art Institute of Chicago, IL. All Rights Reserved. Robert A. Waller Fund: page 72/Gift of Mrs. Albert J. Beveridge in Memory of her Aunt, Delia Spencer Field: page 38/Gift of Mrs. Sterling Morton: page 17/Gift of Mrs. Henry C. Woods: page 121

The Chrysler Museum, Norfolk, VA/Gift of Walter P. Chrysler, Jr.: page 73

Cincinnati Art Museum, OH/John J. Emery Endowment: page 57

Sterling and Francine Clark Art Institute, Williamstown, MA: pages 12(top), 18

The Cleveland Museum of Art, OH/Gift of J. H. Wade: pages 104-105

In the Collection of the Corcoran Gallery of Art, Washington, DC/Museum Purchase, Gallery Fund: page 40

Courtauld Institute Galleries, University of London: pages 13, 47

Dallas Museum of Art, TX/Munger Fund: page 120

The Dayton Art Institute, OH/Gift of Mr. Robert Badenhop: page 9

Denver Art Museum, CO: pages 54-55

© Detroit Institute of Arts, MI/Gift of Dr. Ernest G. Stillman: pages 108-109/Gift of Edward Chandler Walker: pages 88-89

Courtesy, Museum of Fine Arts, Boston, MA/M. Theresa B. Hopkins Fund: pages 36-37/The Hayden Collection: pages 39, 126/Gift of Walter Gay: page 22/Gift of Miss Aimée Lamb in Memory of Mr. and Mrs. Horatio A. Lamb: page 127/Bequest of John T. Spaulding: pages 2, 20

The Fine Arts Museums of San Francisco, CA/Museum Purchase, William H. Noble Bequest Fund: page 56

Flint Institute of Arts, MI/Gift of The Whiting Foundation: pages 44-45

Courtesy of the Fogg Art Museum, Harvard University, Cambridge, MA/Gift of Dr. Ernest G. Stillman: pages 114-15

Glasgow Museums: Art Gallery and Museum, Kelvingrove 2980: pages 50-51

Armand Hammer Collection, U.C.L.A. at Armand Hammer Museum of Art and Cultural Center, Los Angeles, CA: pages 4, 78-79

Collection of Mrs. George Fiske Hammond, Montecito, CA: pages 96-97, 98

Honolulu Academy of Arts, HI/Gift in Memory of Wilhelmina Tenney, 1953 (Photo: Tibor Franyo): page 69

Henry E. Huntington Library and Art Gallery, San Marino, CA: page 119/Virginia Steel Scott Collection: pages 90-91

The Metropolitan Museum of Art, New York, NY/Gift of the Artist, 1923: page 49/Gift of Mrs. Gardner Cassatt, 1965: pages 34-35/Bequest of Mrs H. O. Havemeyer, 1929, The H. O. Havemeyer Collection: pages 99, 106/Bequest of Edith H. Proskauer: page 26/Gift of Mrs. Hope Williams Read, 1962: pages 82-83/Rogers Fund, 1919: page 10, (1918) page 81/Gift of Paul J. Sachs, 1916: page 62, (1917) page 68/From the Collection of James Stillman, Gift of Dr. Ernest G. Stillman, 1922: page 27, 92-93, 94-95

National Gallery of Art, Washington, DC/© 1994 Board of Trustees: pages 76-77/Ailsa Mellon Bruce Collection: page 48/Chester Dale Collection: pages 53, 63, 64, 111 (Photo: Philip A. Charles), page 33/Collection of Mr. and Mrs. Paul Mellon: pages 24-25/Rosenwald Collection: pages 66, 67, 70

National Portrait Gallery, Smithsonian Institution, Washington, DC/Art Resource, New York, NY: page 15

The Nelson-Atkins Museum of Art, Kansas City, MO/Purchase: Acquired through the Generosity of an Anonymous Donor: page 30

From the Collection of the New Britain Museum of American Art, CT/Harriet Russell Stanley Fund (Photo: E. Irving Blomstrand): page 65

The Peabody Institute of the City of Baltimore, on Extended Loan to the Baltimore Museum of Art, MD: page 41

Pennsylvania Academy of Fine Arts, Philadelphia, PA/Archives: pages 6, 7(top)/Gift of John Frederick Lewis: page 7(bottom)

Philadelphia Museum of Art, PA/Gift of Aaron Carpenter: pages 84-85/Given by Charles P. Davis and Gardner Cassatt in Memory of Mary Cassatt: page 12(bottom)/Gift of Margaret Sargent McKean: pages 28-29/Alex Simpson, Jr. Collection: page 118/Gift of the Children of Jean Thompson Thayer: page 21/Given by Mr. and Mrs. Jo Watson Webb: pages 112-13/The W. P. Wilstach Collection: pages 16, 42-43, 47

Photographique de la Réunion des Musées Nationaux, Paris, © Photo R.M.N./Musée d'Orsay: pages 46, 59

Photothèque des Musées de la Ville de Paris, © by SPADEM, 1995/Musée du Petit Palais: pages 19, 31, 32, 124-125

Museo del Prado, Madrid: page 8

Private Collection, Chevy Chase, MD: pages 60-61

Private Collection/Print supplied by Phaidon Press: page 11(bottom)

The Saint Louis Art Museum, MO/Gift of Dr. Ernest G. Stillman: page 117

San Diego Museum of Art, CA/Bequest of Mrs. Henry A. Everett: page 110

Shelburne Museum, Shelburne, VT/Gift of J. Watson Webb, Jr.: page 87

Terra Foundation for the Arts/Daniel J. Terra Collection, Photograph © 1994 Courtesy of Terra Museum of American Art, Chicago, IL: pages 71, 80

Virginia Museum of Fine Arts, Richmond, VA/Gift of an Anonymous Donor: page 75

The Walters Art Gallery, Baltimore, MD: page 107/Bequest of Beatrice A. Kelekian in Memory of Mr. and Mrs. Charles D. Kelekian: page 122

Weidenfeld Archive: page 14

Collection of the Westmorland Museum of Art, Greensburg, PA/Anonymous Gift: page 101

Williams College Museum of Art, Williamstown, MA/On Loan from Dr. Herchel Smith, 1977: page 116